Death by
CHOCOLATE

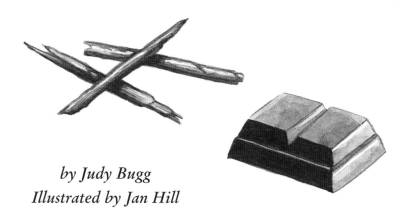

by Judy Bugg
Illustrated by Jan Hill

First published in Great Britain in 1994 by
Parragon Book Service Ltd
Unit 13–17
Avonbridge Trading Estate
Atlantic Road
Avonmouth
Bristol BS11 9QD

ISBN 1 85813 693 8

Edited, designed and typeset by Haldane Mason
Editor: Joanna Swinnerton

Printed in Italy

Note: Cup measurements in this book are for American cups. Tablespoons are assumed to be 15ml. Unless otherwise stated, milk is assumed to be full-fat and eggs are standard size 2.

CONTENTS

CHOCOLATE POTS

SERVES 6

125 g/4 oz/4 squares plain (dark) chocolate

6–8 small fresh rose leaves

150 ml/¼ pint/⅔ cup milk

3 eggs, separated

150 ml/¼ pint/⅔ cup single (light) cream

2 tsp powdered gelatine

2 tbsp orange-flavoured liqueur such as Grand Marnier

150 ml/¼ pint/⅔ cup whipping cream, whipped

Making the chocolate leaves to decorate this dessert can be very therapeutic. Allow plenty of time, and make enough to keep some in reserve. Keep them layered between waxed paper in an airtight container in the refrigerator.

1 Melt the chocolate in a heatproof bowl placed over a saucepan of simmering water. Make sure that the bowl does not touch the bottom of the pan and that water does not splash into the bowl. Coat the waxy side of the rose leaves with melted chocolate, using a clean paint-brush. Leave them on waxed paper to set.

2 Stir the milk into the remaining chocolate and return to the heat, stirring until well mixed. Remove from the heat and whisk in the egg yolks and cream.

3 Dissolve the gelatine in 2 tbsp boiling water until clear. Whisk it into the mousse mixture with the liqueur. Whisk the egg whites until stiff and fold them in. Pour into 6 individual serving cups or ramekins and chill until set.

4 Peel the rose leaves from the chocolate. Pipe a whirl of cream on each cup or ramekin. Just before serving, decorate each one with chocolate leaves.

4

CHOCOLATE PANCAKES

MAKES 12

125 g/4 oz/1 cup plain (all-purpose) flour

pinch of salt

15 g/½ oz/2 tbsp icing (confectioners') sugar

½ tsp mixed spice (apple pie spice)

2 eggs, beaten

300 ml/½ pint/1¼ cups milk

butter for frying

1 quantity Rich Chocolate Sauce (see page 52)

extra icing (confectioners') sugar, sifted, for dusting

single (light) cream to serve

You can make these pancakes ahead of time and keep them layered between sheets of greaseproof paper (baking parchment) in an airtight tin. Warm them in a baking tin (pan) covered with foil just before they are required.

1 Sift the dry ingredients into a bowl and make a well in the centre. Whisk in the eggs and milk to make a smooth pouring batter.

2 Melt a little butter in a 20 cm/8 inch frying pan (skillet) and add enough batter to coat the base thinly and evenly. Cook on both sides until set and light golden brown.

3 Repeat until all the batter is used, layering the pancakes between greaseproof paper (baking parchment), and keeping warm.

4 Drizzle the rich chocolate sauce over each pancake and fold in half and then half again. Place on serving plates and dust with a little extra sifted icing (confectioners') sugar. Serve with a jug of single (light) cream.

6

PROFITEROLES

These are a favourite dessert for almost everyone, and are unbelievably easy to make. Make sure the oven has reached the right temperature, and sprinkle the greased baking sheets with water to make extra steam for perfect choux puffs.

SERVES 8

150 ml/¼ pint/⅔ cup water

60 g/2 oz/¼ cup butter

75 g/2½ oz/½ cup plus 2 tbsp plain (all-purpose) flour, sifted

pinch of salt

2 eggs, beaten

300 ml/½ pint/1¼ cups whipping cream

1 quantity Rich Chocolate Sauce (see page 52)

1 Grease 2 baking sheets lightly and sprinkle with water.

2 Put the water and butter in a saucepan over a low heat until the fat melts, then shoot in the flour and salt. Remove from the heat and beat until the mixture is smooth and leaves the sides of the pan clean.

3 Beat in the eggs a little at a time until thoroughly blended in and the mixture is smooth and glossy.

4 Place in a large piping bag fitted with a large star nozzle (tip) and pipe small whirls, well spaced on the baking sheets.

5 Place in a preheated oven at 200°C, 400°F, Gas Mark 6 and bake for 15–20 minutes until risen and golden. Remove from the oven and slit each choux puff horizontally to allow the steam to escape. Return to the oven for about 5 minutes to dry out slightly. Cool on a wire rack.

6 Whip the cream and use to fill the buns. Pile them in a pyramid shape on a serving plate. Pour the sauce artistically over the buns and serve, or keep them cool until required.

CHOCOLATE AND PISTACHIO BOMBE

This is a really special dessert that involves a bit of cheating, but if you buy good quality homemade-style ice cream, no one will know!

SERVES 8

3 eggs

125 g/4 oz/⅔ cup soft dark brown sugar

100g/3½ oz/¾ cup plus 2 tbsp plain (all-purpose) flour

1½ tbsp cocoa powder

1 tbsp hot water

6 scoops chocolate ice cream

3 scoops vanilla ice cream

3 tbsp shelled, chopped pistachio nuts

1 quantity Rich Chocolate Sauce (optional, see page 52)

1 Grease and line the base of a 33 x 23 cm/13 x 9 inch Swiss (jelly) roll tin (pan) with grease-proof paper (baking parchment).

2 Whisk the eggs and sugar until thick enough to hold the trail of the whisk.

3 Sift the flour and cocoa together and fold half of it into the eggs and sugar. Fold in the water and the rest of the flour mixture and pour into the tin (pan). Tip gently from side to side to level the mixture.

4 Place in a preheated oven at 220°C, 425°F, Gas Mark 7 and bake for 8 minutes. Leave to cool in the tin (pan).

5 When cool, turn the sponge out of the tin (pan). Peel off the paper. Line a large pudding basin with clingfilm (plastic wrap), leaving enough overlap at the top to lift out the bombe when set. Use two thirds of the sponge to line the basin.

6 Beat the chocolate ice cream until slightly soft but still stiff, place half in the basin and press down. Mix the vanilla ice cream with the nuts and add to the basin, pressing down. Cover with the remaining chocolate ice cream and smooth over. Cover with the remaining sponge and trim the edges. Press down well

10

and wrap with clingfilm (plastic wrap). Freeze overnight.

7 To serve, unwrap and then lift the clingfilm (plastic wrap) in the bowl to release the bombe.

Remove the wrapping and stand the bombe in the refrigerator for 1 hour before serving. Cut into slices like a cake and serve with rich chocolate sauce if wished.

TWO-TONE TERRINE

Serve this terrine with a vanilla custard thinned down with orange juice and single (light) cream, and perhaps with a dash of orange-flavoured liqueur. Decorate with rolls of Chocolate Caraque (page 56).

1 Sprinkle the gelatine over 3 tbsp cold water in a bowl.

2 Melt the plain (dark) chocolate and the chocolate buttons separately in two bowls placed over saucepans of simmering water. Make sure the bowl does not touch the bottom of the pan and that water does not splash into the bowl.

3 Blend the egg yolks with the cornflour (cornstarch) in a saucepan and whisk in the cream, milk and sugar. Bring to the boil and stir until smooth and thickened. Divide the mixture between 2 bowls and mix the melted plain (dark) chocolate and liqueur into one and the melted white chocolate buttons into the other.

4 Dissolve the gelatine in a bowl over a saucepan of hot water, and mix half into each bowl of chocolate mixture. Whisk the egg whites until stiff and fold half into each bowl.

5 Pour the white mousse into a 1.75 litre/3 pint/2 quart mould and freeze for 20 minutes until just firm. Add the plain chocolate mousse and smooth over. Chill until set.

6 To serve, loosen the edges with a knife and dip the mould into very hot water for a few seconds. Place a serving plate on top and turn out.

LITTLE CHOCOLATE SOUFFLES

SERVES 8

125 g/4 oz/4 squares plain (dark) chocolate

150 ml/¼ pint/⅔ cup double (heavy) cream

4 eggs, separated

1 tbsp coffee flavouring (extract)

pinch of cream of tartar

4 tbsp icing (confectioners') sugar

single (light) cream to serve

People often think that soufflés are a nightmare to make, but the trick is to chill the mixture overnight or for a few hours. Then all you have to do is pop the soufflés in the oven when the main course has been cleared away.

1 Grease 8 individual soufflé or ramekin dishes.

2 Melt the chocolate in a heatproof bowl placed over a saucepan of simmering water. Make sure that the bowl does not touch the bottom of the pan and that water does not splash into the bowl. Stir in the cream until smooth. Remove from the heat and beat in the egg yolks and coffee flavouring (extract).

3 Whisk the egg whites and cream of tartar until stiff. Whisk in 2 tbsp of the icing (confectioners') sugar. Fold the egg whites into the chocolate mixture and pour gently into the prepared dishes. Cover with clingfilm (plastic wrap) and chill until required.

4 One hour before they are needed, remove the soufflés from the refrigerator and bring to room temperature. Place in a preheated oven at 220°C, 425°F, Gas Mark 7. Bake for 10–15 minutes until well risen and set. Dust with the remaining icing (confectioners') sugar and serve

Little Chocolate Soufflés

on dessert plates with a jug of cream. Breaking a hole in the top of the soufflé and pouring in a little cream is a particularly good way to eat these; it also stops you burning your mouth in hasty anticipation.

BAKED CHOCOLATE CHEESECAKE

A slice of this with a freshly made cappuccino is a real luxury. It is equally delicious as a dessert, served with a little pouring cream.

SERVES 6

200 g/7 oz/1³/₄ cups plain (all-purpose) flour

½ tsp ground cinnamon

90 g/3 oz/⅓ cup softened butter

150 g/5 oz/⅔ cup caster (superfine) sugar

4 eggs plus 4 egg yolks

2½ tsp vanilla flavouring (extract)

200 g/7 oz/1 scant cup curd (low-fat soft) cheese

450 ml/¾ pint/2 cups sour cream

125 g/4 oz/4 squares plain (dark) chocolate, melted

30 g/1 oz/¼ cup cornflour (cornstarch)

TOPPING

double (heavy) cream and crème fraîche (see step 5) and Chocolate Caraque (see page 56)

1 Grease a 23 cm/9 inch loose-bottomed springform tin (pan).

2 To make the pastry, tip the flour on to a cool work surface (counter) and make a well in the centre. Add the cinnamon, butter, 90 g/3 oz/⅓ cup plus 1 tbsp of the sugar, the 4 beaten egg yolks, ½ tsp of the vanilla flavouring (extract) and ½ tsp salt and knead together until smooth. Roll out and use to line the tin (pan).

3 To make the filling, separate the eggs, then whisk the egg yolks and the remaining sugar together with the whisk. Whisk the cheese, cream, melted chocolate, cornflour (cornstarch) and 2 tsp of the vanilla flavouring (extract) together and fold into the egg yolk mixture. Whisk the egg whites until stiff and fold in. Pour into the tin (pan) carefully.

4 Place in a preheated oven at 200°C, 400°F, Gas Mark 6. Bake for 1 hour until set. Leave to cool in the tin (pan) – it will sink as it cools.

5 To decorate, whip 150 ml/¼ pint/⅔ cup double (heavy) cream together with 150 ml/

¼ pint/⅔ cup crème fraîche until thick and spread roughly on top of the cheesecake. Arrange some chocolate caraque on top. Keep cool until required.

STEAMED MOCHA PUDDING

Either Rich Chocolate Sauce (page 52) or Chocolate Custard (page 54) would make the perfect accompaniment to this satisfying pudding. Serve each portion surrounded by a pool of sauce or custard, with Chocolate Caraque (page 56) on the side to decorate.

1 Grease a 900 ml/1¹⁄₂ pt/3¹⁄₂ cup pudding basin and cover the base with a round of greased greaseproof paper (baking parchment).

2 Half fill a large saucepan with water. Stand a trivet in the base of the pan and bring the water to the boil.

3 Cream the butter and sugar together until pale and fluffy. Beat in the eggs gradually. Sift together the cocoa powder, baking powder and flour and fold into the creamed mixture.

4 Dissolve the coffee granules in the boiling water and add to the mixture. Fold in gently but thoroughly, moistening with a little milk if necessary to give a dropping consistency.

5 Spoon into the pudding basin until two thirds full. Level the top and cover

18

the basin with a piece of greased foil, tied tightly on to the basin.

6 Steam for 1½–2 hours, topping up with boiling water when necessary. Never let the pan boil dry. Remove the foil and turn the pudding out carefully on to a serving plate. Serve with your chosen sauce and some chocolate caraque.

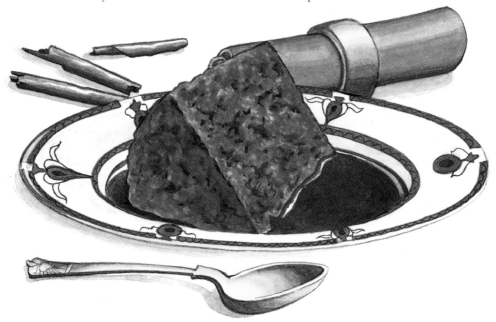

19

CHOCOLATE CHESTNUT ROULADE

This rich, nutty roulade freezes well. Open-freeze, then wrap and keep frozen. Allow about 3 hours for it to defrost, then decorate with whipped cream and marrons glacés.

SERVES 8

150 g/5 oz/5 squares plain (dark) chocolate

5 eggs, separated

175 g/6 oz/1 cup soft light brown sugar

3 tbsp hot water

1 tbsp caster (superfine) sugar

marrons glacés to decorate

FILLING

175 g/6 oz/scant ¾ cup sweetened chestnut purée

300 ml/½ pint/1¼ cups whipping cream

2 tbsp brandy

1 Grease and line the base of a large Swiss (jelly) roll tin (pan) with greaseproof paper (baking parchment).

2 Melt the chocolate in a heatproof bowl over a saucepan of simmering water.

3 Whisk the egg yolks and brown sugar until thick enough to hold the trail of the whisk. Blend the hot water with the melted chocolate and mix gently into the egg mixture.

4 Whisk the egg whites until stiff and fold in to the egg mixture. Pour into the tin (pan) and tip from side to side to level.

5 Bake in a preheated oven at 200°C, 400°F, Gas Mark 6 for 15 minutes. Cool in the tin (pan) for 10 minutes, then cover with a damp tea towel (dish cloth) and leave to rest for 10 minutes.

6 To make the filling, beat the chestnut purée until smooth and add half the cream. Whisk until thick.

7 Sprinkle caster (superfine) sugar over a sheet of greaseproof paper (baking parchment). Turn the roulade on to it and peel off the paper (parchment) it was cooked on. Spread the filling over the roulade, roll up

20

from the long edge and place seam side down on the serving plate. Whisk the remaining cream and brandy until stiff enough to hold its shape. Pipe it along the top of the roulade and decorate with marrons glacés .

CHOCOLATE FUDGE CAKE

Thin slices of this very rich and irresistible cake, served with a little pouring cream, make an unforgettable end to almost any meal.

SERVES 6

90 g/3 oz/3 squares plain (dark) chocolate

175 g/6 oz/¾ cup butter

300 g/10 oz/1⅔ cups soft light brown sugar

2 eggs, beaten

150 ml/¼ pint/⅔ cup boiling water

300 g/10 oz/2½ cups plain (all-purpose) flour sifted

1½ tsp bicarbonate of soda (baking soda)

1 tsp baking powder

150 ml/¼ pint/⅔ cup soured cream

1 tsp vanilla flavouring (extract)

1 quantity Chocolate Fudge Icing (Frosting) (see page 62)

1 Grease and line the bases of 3 x 20 cm/8 inch loose-bottomed sandwich tins (layer pans) with greaseproof paper (baking parchment).

2 Melt the chocolate in a heatproof bowl placed over a saucepan of simmering water. Make sure that the bowl does not touch the bottom of the pan and that water does not splash into the bowl.

3 Cream the butter and the brown sugar together until light and fluffy, then beat in the eggs gradually.

4 Beat the melted chocolate and boiling water together, leave to cool slightly, then mix into the creamed mixture.

5 Sift the flour, bicarbonate of soda (baking soda) and baking powder together and fold into the chocolate mixture alternately with the soured cream and the vanilla flavouring (extract). Divide the mixture between the tins (pans). Bake in a preheated oven at 190°C, 375°F, Gas Mark 5 for 25 minutes. Cool in the tins (pans).

6 Turn out the layers and use the chocolate fudge icing (frosting) to sandwich them together and to coat the top and sides of the cake. Keep cool until required.

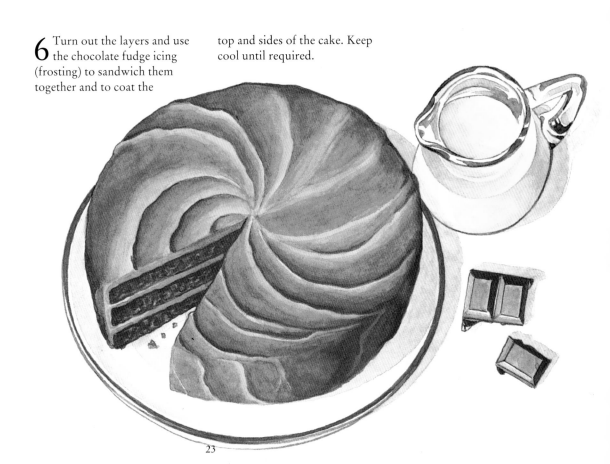

23

CHOCOLATE REFRIGERATOR CAKE

SERVES 8

350 g/12 oz/12 squares plain (dark) chocolate

4 tbsp strong black coffee

4 tbsp brandy

250 g/8 oz digestive biscuits (graham crackers), broken

90 g/3 oz/¾ cup toasted, slivered (flaked) almonds

90 g/3 oz/⅓ cup glacé (candied) cherries

300 ml/½ pint/1¼ cups double (heavy) cream

½ quantity Chocolate Caraque (see page 56)

As there is no cooking involved in making this cake, it is easy and fun for children to make and yet it still looks impressive served as a dessert.

1 Grease an 18 cm/7 inch round loose-bottomed cake tin (pan).

2 Melt the chocolate with the coffee in a heatproof bowl placed over a saucepan of simmering water. Make sure the bowl does not touch the bottom of the pan and that water does not splash into the bowl.

3 Remove from the heat and stir in the brandy, biscuits (crackers), almonds and glacé (candied) cherries.

4 Pour the mixture into the prepared tin (pan) and smooth the top. Chill overnight.

5 Turn out on to a serving plate. Whip the cream until just stiff and pipe it over the top of the cake. Decorate with the chocolate caraque.

CHOCOLATE RUM RING

For this recipe you will need a 'Kugelhopf' or ring mould for the best effect.

SERVES 10

2 tbsp soft light brown sugar

1 tbsp coffee granules

125 g/4 oz/²⁄₃ cup raisins

125 g/4 oz/¹⁄₂ cup dried pears, sliced

3 tbsp dark rum

60 g/2 oz/2 squares plain (dark) chocolate

2 tbsp milk

175 g/6 oz/³⁄₄ cup butter

175 g/6 oz/³⁄₄ cup caster (superfine) sugar

3 eggs, beaten

250 g/8 oz/2 cups self-raising flour

pinch of salt

1 tbsp cocoa powder

300 ml/¹⁄₂ pint/1¹⁄₄ cups whipping cream

1 Grease and flour a 1.25 litre/2 pint/5 cup ring mould.

2 Put the brown sugar, coffee, raisins and dried pear slices with 450 ml/¾ pint/scant 2 cups of boiling water in a saucepan. Cook over a low heat until the sugar dissolves, then boil for 2 minutes. Remove from the heat and stir in the rum. Leave to cool.

3 Melt the chocolate in a heatproof bowl placed over a saucepan of simmering water. Make sure that the bowl does not touch the bottom of the pan and that water does not splash into the bowl.

4 Blend the chocolate and milk together until smooth over a low heat. Cream the butter and sugar together and beat in the eggs gradually. Stir the chocolate mixture into the creamed mixture. Sift the flour, salt and cocoa together and fold into the mixture. Spoon into the ring mould and smooth over.

5 Place in a preheated oven at 180°C, 350°F, Gas Mark 4 and bake for 30–35 minutes. Leave to cool for 5 minutes, then turn out on to a wire rack and leave to cool completely.

6 Return the cake to the clean ring mould and pierce with a skewer. Drain the fruit and reserve. Pour the liquid over the cake until soaked. Chill for several hours.

7 Turn out on to a serving plate and fill the centre with the fruit. Whip the cream and pipe it around the base of the ring before serving.

BLACK FOREST GATEAU

This rich gâteau is one of the most popular desserts around. This version is the real thing, and really is more a cake than a dessert. Using the whole marinated cherries with stalks adds grandeur, and makes this cake perfect to bring out at celebrations.

SERVES 6

60 g/2 oz/¼ cup unsalted butter

75 g/2½ oz/½ cup plus 2 tbsp plain (all-purpose) flour, sifted

15 g/½ oz/2 tbsp cornflour (cornstarch), sifted

30 g/1 oz/¼ cup cocoa powder

4 eggs

125 g/4 oz/½ cup caster (superfine) sugar

475 g/15 oz can stoned (pitted) morello or black cherries

1 tbsp arrowroot

3 tbsp clear cherry liqueur

450 ml/¾ pint/scant 2 cups whipping cream

60 g/2 oz/2 squares plain (dark) chocolate, grated

8–10 fresh or whole cherries marinated in syrup, with stalks

1 Grease and line a 20 cm/ 8 inch loose-bottomed cake tin (pan).

2 Melt the butter and leave to cool. Sift the flour, cornflour (cornstarch) and cocoa powder together twice.

3 Whisk the eggs and sugar until pale and thick enough to hold the trail of the whisk. Fold in the butter and the flour mixture gently, a little at a time.

4 Pour into the tin (pan) and place in a preheated oven at 190°C, 375°F, Gas Mark 5, and bake for 20–25 minutes, until firm to the touch.

5 Turn the cake out of the tin (pan) and cool on a wire rack. Split into 3 equal layers.

6 Drain the liquid from the canned cherries into a bowl and make up the liquid to 150 ml/¼ pint/⅔ cup with water if necessary. Blend a little of the liquid with the arrowroot and add the remaining liquid. Transfer to a saucepan, bring to the boil and cook until thickened and clear. Stir in the cherries and leave to cool.

7 Sprinkle the sponge layers with the liqueur and cover 2 with the cherry mixture. Spread

a third of the cream over these 2 layers. Spread some cream around the sides of the cake. Roll the sides of the cake in the grated chocolate. Spread half the remaining cream on top of the cake and pipe the rest in whirls around the edge. Decorate with the whole cherries with stalks.

SACHERTORTE

SERVES 6

90 g/3 oz/3 squares bitter (semisweet) chocolate

90 g/3 oz/⅓ cup unsalted butter

125 g/4 oz/½ cup caster (superfine) sugar

5 eggs, separated

1 tbsp dark rum

pinch of ground cinnamon

90 g/3 oz/¾ cup toasted hazelnuts, ground

1 quantity Chocolate Ganache (see page 58)

cocoa powder to decorate

This classic Austrian cake is simple and sophisticated. There is no flour in it, as this is replaced with ground hazelnuts. You can either write the word 'Sacher' on top with a little ganache, in true Austrian style, or decorate with stripes of cocoa powder, as described below.

1 Grease and line a 23 cm/ 9 inch loose-bottomed cake tin (pan) with greaseproof paper (baking parchment).

2 Melt the chocolate in a heatproof bowl placed over a saucepan of simmering water.

3 Cream the butter and sugar until smooth and fluffy. Beat in the egg yolks gradually.

4 Add the rum to the melted chocolate, mix until smooth and whisk into the egg mixture. Fold in the cinnamon and hazelnuts. Whisk the egg whites until just stiff and fold into the mixture gently but thoroughly.

Pour into the tin (pan), leaving the mixture to find its own level.

5 Bake in a preheated oven at 200°C, 400°F, Gas Mark 6, for 30 minutes until well risen and the top springs back when lightly pressed. Leave to cool, then remove from the tin (pan). The cake will sink on cooling.

6 Reserve a little chocolate ganache for piping if wished. Pour the rest over the cooled cake, easing it down the sides so that the whole cake is covered smoothly. Leave to set.

7 To decorate, cover the top of the cake with evenly spaced

strips of paper. Dust with cocoa
powder and remove the strips
carefully. Alternatively, use the
reserved ganache to pipe the
word 'Sacher' on top.

FUDGE BROWNIES

These brownies are exceptionally more-ish, mainly because of their slight chewiness. This recipe uses pecan nuts, but you can substitute walnuts. These also make a great dessert with a whirl of whipped cream or a dash of Chocolate Custard (page 54).

MAKES 16

60 g/2 oz/2 squares plain (dark) chocolate

125 g/4 oz/¼ cup butter

2 eggs, beaten

250 g/8 oz/1⅓ cups soft dark brown sugar

1 tsp vanilla flavouring (extract)

90 g/3 oz/¾ cup self-raising flour

90 g/3 oz/¾ cup pecan nuts, broken

1 Grease and line the base of an 18 cm/7 inch, shallow square tin (pan) with greaseproof paper (baking parchment)

2 Melt the chocolate and butter in a heatproof bowl placed over a saucepan of simmering water until smooth.

Make sure the bowl does not touch the bottom of the pan and that water does not splash into the bowl.

3 Whisk the eggs and the sugar together until thick and pale. Fold in the chocolate mixture and vanilla flavouring (extract).

4 Sift in the flour and add the nuts. Fold together gently and pour into the tin (pan).

5 Place on the middle shelf of a preheated oven at 180°C, 350°F, Gas Mark 4 and bake for 40 minutes. Leave to cool in the tin

Fudge Brownies

(pan). The top should look cracked when cool.

6 Turn out and cut into squares or fingers. If you like, add a little extra luxury by dabbing some Chocolate Ganache (see page 58) or melted chocolate on the top of each brownie and topping with a whole pecan nut.

CHOCOLATE FANCIES

These rich chocolate fingers are decorated with piped squiggles of white chocolate, which contrasts well with the dark Chocolate Ganache topping.

SERVES 6

175 g/6 oz/1½ cups plain (all-purpose) flour	
2 tbsp cocoa powder	
1 tsp bicarbonate of soda (baking soda)	
1 tsp baking powder	
60 g/2 oz/½ cup flaked (slivered) almonds	
150 g/5 oz/¾ cup soft dark brown sugar	
2 tbsp golden (light corn) syrup	
2 eggs, beaten	
150 ml/¼ pint/⅔ cup milk	
1 quantity Chocolate Ganache (see page 58)	
125 g/4 oz/⅔ cup white chocolate buttons	

1 Grease and line an 18 cm/7 inch square cake tin (pan) with greaseproof paper (baking parchment).

2 Sift the flour, cocoa powder, bicarbonate of soda (baking soda) and baking powder into a bowl. Make a well in the centre and add the almonds, sugar, syrup, eggs and milk. Beat well to a smooth batter and pour into the tin (pan).

3 Bake in a preheated oven at 160°C, 325°F, Gas Mark 3 for about 1¼ hours until it is firm to the touch and has shrunk away slightly from the edge of the tin (pan). Leave to cool before turning out.

4 Cut into 12 fingers and coat with the chocolate ganache. Leave to set on sheets of greaseproof paper (baking parchment). When the ganache has almost set, melt the white chocolate buttons and use to pipe squiggles on the fingers. Leave to set.

CHOCOLATE CHIP COOKIES

MAKES 20

90 g/3 oz/⅓ cup butter

175 g/6 oz/1 cup soft dark brown sugar

½ tsp vanilla flavouring (extract)

1 egg, beaten

175 g/6 oz/1½ cups self-raising flour

pinch of salt

60 g/2 oz/½ cup walnuts, chopped

90 g/3 oz/½ cup chocolate buttons

Making homemade cookies is easy and really worthwhile, and makes the kitchen smell wonderful! These cookies won't hang around for long as they are extremely more-ish.

1 Cream the butter, sugar and vanilla flavouring (extract) together until thick and fluffy. Beat in the egg gradually.

2 Fold in the flour and salt with the walnuts and chocolate buttons.

3 Place spoonfuls of the mixture well spaced on greased baking sheets. Place in a preheated oven at 180°C, 350°F, Gas Mark 4 and bake for about 15 minutes.

4 Leave to cool on the baking sheets for a few minutes before transferring to wire racks. When cold, store in an airtight tin in a cool place.

FLORENTINES

These florentines make wonderful petits fours. Coat them in white and dark chocolate and arrange on a serving plate, or pack in gift boxes for delicious presents.

MAKES 20

60 g/2 oz/¼ cup butter

60 g/2 oz/¼ cup caster (superfine) sugar

1 tbsp lemon juice

45 g/1½ oz plain (all-purpose) flour

30 g/1 oz/¼ cup flaked (slivered) almonds

60 g/2 oz/½ cup walnuts, chopped

60 g/2 oz/¼ cup coloured glacé (candied) cherries, chopped

30 g/1 oz/3 tbsp mixed peel

30 g/1 oz/3 tbsp sultanas (golden raisins)

2 tbsp single (light) cream

125 g/4 oz/4 squares plain (dark) chocolate or 125 g/4 oz/⅔ cup white chocolate buttons

1 Grease 3 baking sheets lightly and cover with greaseproof paper (baking parchment).

2 Put the butter and sugar into a saucepan over a low heat until the sugar dissolves, then boil for 2 minutes. Leave to cool for 5 minutes.

3 Stir in the remaining ingredients except for the chocolate. Mix well and place small spoonfuls well spaced on the baking sheets.

4 Place one baking sheet at a time in a preheated oven at 180°C, 350°F, Gas Mark 4 and bake for 10 minutes. Remove from the oven and neaten the edges of the florentines with an oiled palette knife. Leave to cool.

5 Melt the plain (dark) chocolate in a bowl placed over a saucepan of simmering water. Make sure that the bowl does not touch the bottom of the pan and that water does not splash into the bowl. Coat the smooth side of each florentine

with the melted chocolate. Place chocolate side up on greaseproof paper (baking parchment) and leave to set. Store in an airtight container in a cool place.

DARK RUM TRUFFLES

These are delicious little treats to serve after dinner. If ginger isn't your favourite flavour, use chocolate cake for this recipe.

1 Put the dates into a saucepan with enough water to cover. Cover and simmer gently for 15 minutes. Remove the lid and cook until all the liquid has evaporated.

2 Put the dates, cake, nuts and liqueur or rum in a bowl and mix thoroughly, or place in a food processor and work until smooth. Chill the mixture until easy to handle.

3 When firm, pinch off pieces and shape into 16 small balls. Melt the chocolate in a heatproof bowl placed over a saucepan of simmering water. Make sure that the bowl does not touch the bottom of the pan and that water does not splash into the bowl. Coat the truffles with melted chocolate and leave to set on sheets of greaseproof paper (baking parchment).

40

4 When set, transfer to paper petits fours cases and store in an airtight container in a cool place.

CHOCOLATE NESTS

MAKES 8

175 g/6 oz/6 squares plain (dark) chocolate

60 g/2 oz/¼ cup butter

3 shredded wheat biscuits

60 g/2 oz/⅓ cup raisins

24 miniature chocolate eggs

This is a real Easter treat for the children and it's so easy to make that they can help. The nest effect is achieved by using breakfast cereal biscuits made of shredded wheat.

1 Lightly grease an 8-serving bun tin (pan).

2 Melt the chocolate and butter in a heatproof bowl placed over a saucepan of simmering water until smooth. Make sure that the bowl does not touch the bottom of the pan and that water does not splash into the bowl.

3 Crumble the shredded wheat biscuits and stir them into the melted chocolate with the raisins until well mixed.

4 Spoon the mixture into the bun tins. Make a depression in the centre of each 'nest' and fill it with miniature chocolate eggs. Chill until set.

CHOCOLATE PEPPERMINT FONDANTS

MAKES 20

5 tsp glycerine

½ egg white, beaten

250 g/8 oz/scant 2 cups icing (confectioners') sugar, sifted

green colouring

peppermint flavouring (extract)

sifted icing (confectioners') sugar for dusting

250 g/8 oz/8 squares plain (dark) chocolate

These peppermints are easy for either children or adults to prepare, and they make ideal treats and gifts. You can jazz them up by adding decorations while the chocolate is still wet, such as whole nuts or crystallized violets.

1 Stir the glycerine and egg white into the sifted icing (confectioners') sugar until well mixed. Add, drop by drop, enough colouring and peppermint flavouring (extract) to colour and flavour to your taste.

2 Lightly dust a work surface (counter) with sifted icing (confectioners') sugar, and knead the peppermint mixture until smooth. Wrap in clingfilm (plastic wrap) and leave to rest overnight.

3 Knead again and roll out to a thickness of 5 mm/¼ inch. Using a 2.5 cm/1 inch plain cutter, cut out rounds and lay on sheets of greaseproof paper (baking parchment).

4 Melt the chocolate in a heatproof bowl placed over a saucepan of simmering water. Make sure the bowl does not touch the bottom of the pan and that water does not splash into the bowl. Dip each peppermint fondant quickly in the melted chocolate. Shake off the excess, then lay carefully on the paper (parchment). Decorate as you like, and leave to set. Place in petits fours cases and pack in boxes or pretty cellophane bags.

APRICOT HARLEQUINS

MAKES 16

125 g/4 oz/²⁄₃ cup dried apricots

125 g/4 oz Madeira (pound) cake, crumbled

2 tbsp clear orange-flavoured liqueur

30 g/1 oz/¼ cup ground almonds

30 g/1 oz flaked (slivered) almonds

250 g/8 oz/1¹⁄₃ cups white chocolate buttons

These unusual petits fours are made with dried fruit, Madeira (pound) cake and nuts, and are satisfyingly chewy as well as sweet. To add a little interest, coat some with white and some with dark (plain) chocolate.

1 Put the apricots in a saucepan with enough water to cover. Cover with a lid and simmer gently for 15 minutes. Remove the apricots from the liquid and set aside.

2 Mix the apricots, cake, liqueur and ground almonds in a food processor until smooth. Mix in the flaked almonds and chill until firm.

3 Pinch off pieces of the mixture and shape into diamonds. Melt the chocolate buttons in a heatproof bowl placed over a saucepan of simmering water. Make sure that the bowl does not touch the bottom of the pan and that water does not splash into the bowl. Dip the apricot harlequins in the melted chocolate until they are coated all over. Leave to set on sheets of greaseproof paper (baking parchment).

4 Place in paper petits fours cases and store in an airtight container in a cool place.

ICED CHOCOLATE MILK SHAKE

SERVES 4

900 ml/1½ pints/3½ cups cold milk

150 ml/¼ pint/⅔ cup Rich Chocolate Sauce (see page 52)

4 scoops chocolate ice cream

1 tsp drinking chocolate powder

If you keep a batch of the rich chocolate sauce base in the refrigerator, these delicious shakes can be whipped up in seconds. A lighter version can be made with low-fat ice cream and semi-skimmed milk.

1 Whisk the milk and cold chocolate sauce vigorously, or mix in a blender, until the liquid is frothy and well blended.

2 Pour into 4 tall glasses. Place a scoop of ice cream carefully on top of each drink so that it floats and dust with a little powdered drinking chocolate. Serve with long straws, and with spoons to eat the froth and ice cream at the end.

50

RICH CHOCOLATE SAUCE

This sauce is delicious poured over almost anything: choux buns, ice cream, fresh fruit, desserts and even cakes. It can be poured over poached pears to make Poires Belle Hélène, or over bananas and cream for a banana split. It will keep, chilled, for up to a week.

MAKES 600 ml/ 1 pint/2½ cups

250 g/8 oz/8 squares bitter (semisweet) chocolate

2 tbsp golden (light corn) syrup

2 tbsp coffee flavouring (extract)

300 ml/½ pint/1¼ cups single (light) cream

2 tbsp dark rum

1 Break the chocolate into a heavy-based saucepan and add the syrup, coffee flavouring (extract) and cream. Stir over a low heat until smooth and glossy.

2 Stir in the rum and leave to cool. The sauce will thicken as it cools.

3 Keep in an airtight container in the refrigerator for up to a week. Warm the sauce through gently before serving.

CHOCOLATE CUSTARD

Everybody loves real custard, so try this homemade chocolate custard for a change. It is especially good with steamed puddings. If cooled, it can be used as a base for homemade ice cream.

MAKES 600 ml/ 1 pint/2½ cups

3 egg yolks

30 g/1 oz/1½ tbsp soft light brown sugar

1 tsp vanilla flavouring (extract)

1 tbsp cornflour (cornstarch)

2 tbsp cocoa powder

450 ml/¾ pint/scant 2 cups milk

1 Blend the egg yolks, sugar, vanilla flavouring (extract), cornflour (cornstarch) and cocoa powder with enough milk to make a smooth paste.

2 Heat the remaining milk to boiling point, then whisk into the creamed egg mixture very slowly. Return the mixture to the saucepan and stir over a low heat until the custard thickens, making sure it doesn't catch on the bottom of the pan. Pour into a jug and serve warm.

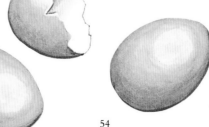

CHOCOLATE CARAQUE

175 g/6 oz/6 squares plain (dark) chocolate

These scrolls of chocolate will add a professional touch to any gâteau or dessert. It takes a bit of practice, but it is well worth the effort. If you make more than you need, it will keep in layers of waxed paper in an airtight container in the refrigerator.

1 Chill a large marble slab or smooth wooden board. Melt the chocolate in a heatproof bowl placed over a saucepan of simmering water. Make sure the bowl does not touch the bottom of the pan and that water does not splash into the bowl.

2 Pour the melted chocolate on to the marble or board and smooth out to a depth of 5 mm/¼ inch. Leave to set. The chocolate can be chilled in the refrigerator, but don't leave it for too long, as it should be firm but not hard.

3 Hold a long-bladed knife firmly at an angle of 45° to the marble or board and push the blade away from you slowly, cutting into the chocolate to make scrolls. Adjust the angle if necessary (it may take a few practice runs before they come out right). Use a cocktail stick (toothpick) to lift the scrolls on to greaseproof paper (baking parchment). Keep the caraque chilled until required.

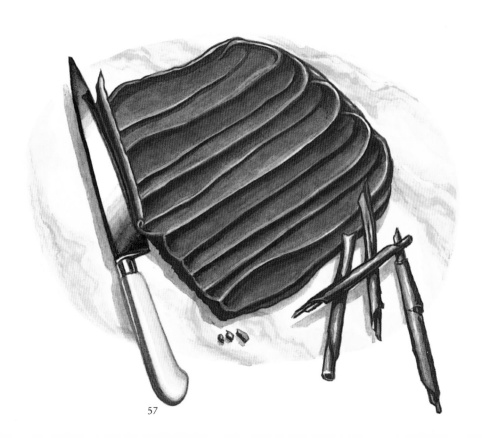

CHOCOLATE GANACHE

This silky smooth chocolate coating is quick and easy, and suitable for all kinds of cake. Once the ganache has set, the cake's keeping qualities are improved if it is stored in a cool place. This amount will coat a 23 cm/9 inch cake or 12 fingers.

175 g/6 oz/6 squares bitter (semisweet) chocolate

150 ml/¼ pint/⅔ cup double (heavy) cream

1 Melt the chocolate in a heatproof bowl placed over a saucepan of simmering water. Make sure that the bowl does not touch the bottom of the pan and the water does not splash into the bowl. Stir the chocolate until smooth.

2 Remove the pan from the heat and whisk the cream into the melted chocolate.

Whisk or stir until the mixture cools and thickens slightly.

3 Pour over the cake carefully so that a smooth finish is achieved over the top and sides.

CHOCOLATE CREME AU BEURRE

This is a simple filling that can be used in numerous ways: for example, you could use it to jazz up a coffee cake or to fill a plain Swiss (jelly) roll. This will make enough to top and fill a 20–23 cm/8–9 inch cake.

60 g/2 oz/2 squares bitter (semisweet) chocolate, melted

90 g/3 oz/⅓ cup caster (superfine) sugar

5 tbsp water

3 egg yolks

175 g/6 oz/¾ cup unsalted butter, diced

1 Melt the chocolate in a heatproof bowl placed over a saucepan of simmering water. Make sure that the bowl does not touch the bottom of the pan and that water does not splash into the bowl.

2 Put the sugar and water in a heavy-based saucepan over a low heat until the sugar has dissolved – do not let the mixture boil.

3 When the liquid is clear, bring to the boil and boil for 2–3 minutes or until the syrup reaches 110°C/225°F on a sugar thermometer.

4 Whisk the egg yolks until frothy and then whisk in the syrup in a steady stream. Whisk in the melted chocolate, and keep whisking until the mixture has cooled.

5 Beat the butter until smooth and then whisk in the chocolate syrup. Use to fill and top the chosen cake.

CHOCOLATE FUDGE ICING (FROSTING)

175 g/6 oz/6 squares plain (dark) chocolate

60 g/2 oz/¼ cup butter

300 g/10 oz/2¼ cups icing (confectioners' sugar), sifted

½ tsp vanilla flavouring (extract)

1 tbsp glycerine

Traditionally used to fill and cover Devil's Food Cake, this rich velvety icing (frosting) is a must for any kind of chocolate cake, especially if you want a moist filling. This will top and fill a 20 cm/8 inch cake.

1 Heat the butter and chocolate together in a heatproof bowl placed over a saucepan of simmering water. Make sure that the bowl does not touch the bottom of the pan and that water does not splash into the bowl.

2 Remove from the heat and beat in 2 tbsp water, the icing (confectioners') sugar, vanilla flavouring (extract) and the glycerine.

3 Leave the icing (frosting) to cool until it has thickened

but is still malleable. Use to fill and coat the cake of your choice. It is easiest to spread it with a large, flat-bladed knife such as a palette knife, or with the back of a large spoon.